Rick Monson.

For more information about Genos
Emotional Intelligence Assessments and
Trainings:

570-517-7100
rick@paramountbusinessdevelopment.com
admin@paramountbusinessdevelopment.com
paramountbusinessdevelopment.com

Helping businesses
reach New HEIGHTS.

THE
Emotionally
Intelligent
LEADER

THE MISSING INGREDIENT
FOR LEADERSHIP SUCCESS

DAVID. R. SMITH

BALBOA.
PRESS
A DIVISION OF HAY HOUSE

Balboa Press books may be ordered through booksellers or by contacting:

Balboa Press
A Division of Hay House
1663 Liberty Drive
Bloomington, IN 47403
www.balboapress.com.au
1 (877) 407-4847

Because of the dynamic nature of the Internet, any web addresses or
links contained in this book may have changed since publication and
may no longer be valid. The views expressed in this work are solely those
of the author and do not necessarily reflect the views of the publisher,
and the publisher hereby disclaims any responsibility for them.

The author of this book does not dispense medical advice or prescribe the use
of any technique as a form of treatment for physical, emotional, or medical
problems without the advice of a physician, either directly or indirectly. The
intent of the author is only to offer information of a general nature to help
you in your quest for emotional and spiritual well-being. In the event you use
any of the information in this book for yourself, which is your constitutional
right, the author and the publisher assume no responsibility for your actions.

Any people depicted in stock imagery provided by Thinkstock are
models, and such images are being used for illustrative purposes only.
Certain stock imagery © Thinkstock.

Print information available on the last page.

ISBN: 978-1-5043-0967-7 (sc)
ISBN: 978-1-5043-0966-0 (e)

Balboa Press rev. date: 08/23/2017

To my parents
for giving me the opportunity to follow my dreams
To my wife
for making these dreams come true

ACKNOWLEDGEMENT

I had a light bulb moment two years ago, having read Daniel Goleman's book, *Emotional Intelligence: Why It Can Matter More than IQ* for the third time. It refers to people being motivated by the need for achievement or the need to help others. When I reflected on all my roles to date and my life experiences, it was clear that my motivation was the latter and hence the stimulus to write this book. I couldn't have done it by myself - I would like to thank those who have supported my ambitions over the years.

Firstly, thank you to my three treasures in life, my wife Gayle, my two children Hazel and Max, who inspire me to challenge my assumptions and give me the opportunity to think outside the world I live in. A huge thanks to Louise, without her and HR Coach providing the platform for my endeavours, none of this would have become a reality. Thanks to Ben, the Genos team, Jill, Josh and James, who provide me with the tools and opportunity to inspire and help others. And finally, to Eileen, who provided me with the courage to be who I wanted to be, and Sue who said once upon a time I had a book in me......

Helping professionals apply core emotional intelligence skills that enhance their self-awareness, empathy, leadership, and resilience.

FOREWORD BY DR BEN PALMER, CEO, GENOS INTERNATIONAL

I first met David in November 2012, on one of our Emotional Intelligence Certification programs. With a bunch of his colleagues, we explored the Genos model and measures of emotional intelligence and how best to use them in personal and team development. Since that time, David and I have worked closely together on a broad range of emotional intelligence development projects and I now engage David regularly to debrief our clients on their assessment results.

What David does really well is explain what emotional intelligence is, why it's important and the steps people can take to enhance it within themselves. And that's exactly what this book does. In a clear, accessible, practical and engaging way, David has brought emotional intelligence, and how to apply it in leadership, to life.

The fact that David has brought the Genos model to life is particularly close to my heart. I designed this model together with Professor Con Stough and Dr Gilles Gignac at Swinburne University as part of my PhD project. I've spent the better part of a decade researching how best to define emotional intelligence and it's dimensions. In this book, David has articulated it in a really meaningful way.

One the things I love most about emotional intelligence is that it can be developed and the development of it positively impacts how we make decisions, how we engage, communicate and collaborate with others, and how we perform. Importantly in leadership it makes a big different to how we influence others and the motivation and performance of those we lead. If you are looking to improve your leadership impact, influence and resilience I couldn't think of a better book to read.

PROLOGUE

The emotionally intelligent leader sat down at his desk, looked out across the city landscape and breathed out contentedly. This had been an amazing journey, but the sense of satisfaction that he was now experiencing had made that journey all the more rewarding.

He took one last look at the latest employee engagement scores and smiled. Productivity was up, performance had improved and the organisation was at last exceeding even his expectations. He shut the report and put it in his desk drawer, closed his eyes and reflected on how this had come to pass. At last he was now running a great organisation.

This is his story.

CHAPTER 1

What Is Emotional Intelligence?

I was sitting in my office, looking at the forecast results for the end of the financial year. The organisation was not performing to expectation; productivity was good, but not great, and overall, staff did not seem to be engaged in the business. They appeared to be simply just doing enough. I had empowered my leadership team to drive the organisation, but although they were smart people and worked hard, they seem to be lacking the necessary skills to lead and motivate their teams to perform. There was one ingredient missing.

Over the past twelve months, I had sent my leadership team to several highly regarded development courses, but they had no enduring impact and had proved to be expensive, with little or no return on investment. Performance did improve initially, but after the enthusiasm from the learning dissipated, it soon returned to business as usual. Something had to change; this organisation had the potential to be great. I had tried everything.

Or so I thought.

I then remembered reading an article in a leadership journal that referred to a successful leader as emotionally intelligent, and how he had used emotional intelligence to inspire performance and create a highly engaged workforce capable of delivering exceptional results. I searched on the Internet and found the article. The person in question, Andrew Miles, was less than an hour's drive away, I picked up the phone and put in a call to the man they referred to as the emotionally intelligent leader.

Trudi, Andrew's secretary put me through to him immediately. I explained that I had read the article and was intrigued as to how emotional intelligence was helping to drive performance and achieve great results for his organisation.

"I can understand why you are intrigued," responded Andrew. "When I was first exposed to the concept of emotional intelligence, I dismissed it without consideration. How many leaders do you know who talk openly about how they feel and consider the feelings of others? It stuck in my mind, though, and eventually, I made the decision to explore it further. I had nothing to lose and wanted to see if it was all that it was being purported to be."

He continued, "I am so thankful I did. It has changed the way I conduct myself in both my work and personal life in such a way, I feel I need to share my experience. I have some time free tomorrow morning. Why don't you come in at ten o'clock, and I'll explain how I came to be known as an emotionally intelligent leader."

"I would really appreciate that," I replied. "I look forward to seeing you tomorrow at ten."

Having taken the plunge, I was still unsure if this was the right solution for me. *Don't die wondering*, I thought, and promised myself I would go in with an open mind and leave my scepticism at the door.

I arrived at the premises early the following morning, was escorted to Andrew's office, and was greeted by the emotionally intelligent leader himself. He was not quite what I expected.

"We are a bit pushed for time," Andrew said, "so with your permission, I would like to get straight into why you are here, which I believe is to get a clearer understanding of how emotional intelligence can assist you, your leadership team, and your employees improve performance, from both an individual and an organisational perspective."

"That's pretty much it in a nutshell," I replied. "I have investigated and implemented a number of initiatives, but they had limited impact. I found the article interesting, and it got my attention. However, I wanted to find out more before I waste money on something I had no real understanding of."

"Well, it certainly has been a game changer for me and my organisation," Andrew said enthusiastically. "Let me take a step back, though, and share with you a simple formula I have been using to drive success for a number of years now, albeit ineffectively, based on what I know now."

He showed me a quote in a frame with a picture below it.

Nothing in the world can take the place of persistence. Talent will not. There is nothing more common that unsuccessful people with talent. A successful person is one who puts in 100 percent physical, mental, and emotional effort.

—Calvin Coolidge

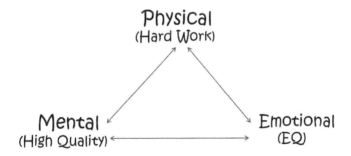

"I have used this model for a number of years," he explained. "Physical. Mental. Emotional. Physical effort is related to the amount of hard work we put in as individuals. The hours we work. Mental effort is the quality of the work we produce over a period of time. Can we remain focused and deliver consistently high outcomes? Emotional effort is how we manage our emotions to ensure we work hard and deliver high-quality results on a more frequent basis. I was aware of how our emotions affected both the physical and mental aspects of work, which ultimately affected performance, but had no idea why. I started reading research based on the concept of emotional intelligence. Let me share what I discovered.

"Emotional intelligence was originally defined in a 1990 article by Peter Salovey, dean of psychology at Yale University, and Jack Meyer, from the University of New Hampshire. In their article, they suggested that there might be abilities that have to do with emotions just as there are with words, numbers, or shapes. They also proposed that individuals differed in emotional abilities and that these abilities may be important because they could be developed and could underpin many important areas of life, such as success at work and the quality of interpersonal relationships.

"It was these latter concepts that caught the attention of Daniel Goleman. It was this connection between emotional intelligence and decisions, and between behaviour and performance, that inspired him to write a book that placed particular emphasis on the links between emotional intelligence and important life criteria. Daniel's first book, *Emotional Intelligence: Why It Can Matter More than IQ,* brought widespread attention to the topic and resulted in the emergence of a number of different models and measures of emotional intelligence.

"I looked at a number of these models but was finding it hard to determine which model was right for my specific need. I was then introduced to a Dr. Ben Palmer, founder of genos. His PhD thesis looked at these different models and measures; he developed a common and definitive approach to defining and measuring emotional intelligence and how this applied to leadership."

Andrew handed me a framed print with the genos definition of emotional intelligence and the model with six competencies.

"Emotional Intelligence is a set of skills that define how effectively we perceive, understand, express reason with and manage our own emotions, and the emotions of others."

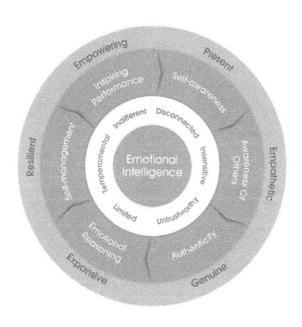

"This was the definition that caught my attention, and the competencies of the model captured the leadership skills and behaviours critical to leadership performance that manifest from emotional intelligence abilities. So I was interested to understand when emotional intelligence was applied to leadership, what impact it would have on my organisation's performance. Let me explain further," he said.

"As you can see, the model consists of six distinct competencies:

- emotional self-awareness
- emotional awareness of others
- authenticity
- emotional reasoning
- emotional self-management
- inspiring performance"

Andrew pointed to the model and said, "At the centre of the model is emotional intelligence, as emotionally intelligent leadership competencies are based on emotional intelligence. Our emotions influence decisions, behaviour, and performance, productively and unproductively. Research shows that there is a direct link between the way people feel and how they perform in the workplace. Applied in leadership, emotional intelligence is about how intelligently you use your emotions to inspire performance in others to deliver great results.

"With the genos tool, our goal is to increase the frequency of the outer circle *productive* leadership being states. We need to be present with our emotions and conscious of how they are impacting our decisions, behaviours, and performance and how we impact those we interact with. We need to be empathetic towards others and understand what makes them feel specific emotions, be authentic in our expression, and use emotional data to make expansive decisions and build resilience to manage and control our emotions and inspire performance in others."

I nodded.

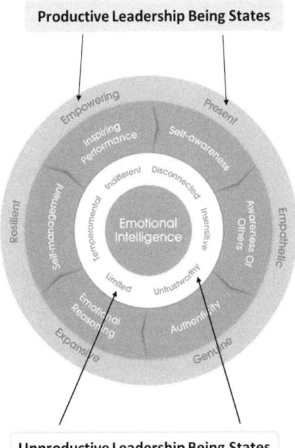

'Genos Model Of Emotionally Intelligent
Leadership Competencies'

Andrew continued, "At the same time, we must also aim to reduce the frequency of the inner circle, *unproductive* leadership being states, with the knowledge that we all spend time displaying the inner circle behaviours. When we are disconnected from our emotions, we are unaware of how they are impacting our decisions, behaviours, and performance. We are insensitive to the emotions of others and don't care how they feel. We are guarded in how we express our emotions and seen to be untrustworthy. We make limited decisions, are seen to be temperamental and unable to manage our emotions, and are indifferent towards others, creating a negative environment in which to work."

I turned, looked at the model, and then said, "This is all well and good, but from my understanding, all this emotion stuff is a bit wishy-washy, isn't it? I mean, surely showing your emotions in the workplace is perceived as a weakness?"

Andrew sighed. "A lot of leaders believe that, to their detriment. However, you must have felt some emotion that compelled you to pick up the phone and ring me, didn't you? Maybe not. And therein lies the problem. If we aren't aware of our own emotions, how do we know how they are impacting what we do on a day-to-day basis, individually and as a leader?"

That was something I hadn't considered. Andrew shared more detail.

"Self-awareness is the foundation of the model. People who are emotionally self-aware are conscious of the role their feelings can play and are better equipped to manage this influence effectively. When we are emotionally self-aware, we are present with the role feelings are playing in our decisions, behaviour, and performance and the subsequent effect we have on others. When we started to focus on our leaders' emotional capability, that's when the performance turned around," he concluded.

"So how do I become more aware of my emotions and the impact they are having on my performance?" I asked eagerly.

"That's a good question," he replied, "but one that you need to find out for yourself. I sensed from our conversation on the phone that you are feeling a little disappointed about the performance of your organisation and see emotional intelligence as a potential solution to drive a high-performance culture."

"Based on my readings and this conversation, I am hoping that is the case," I replied, smiling.

"Great. I am glad to see that you are still keeping an open mind. I have arranged for you to meet with some of my leadership team, who practice the concept of emotional intelligence and saw significant improvement as a result."

"What sort of improvement?" I asked.

"I'll leave that for them to explain. My personal assistant has a list of people I suggest you talk to. Your first meeting is with Gayle Ferguson, our general manager, at eleven. She is expecting you. When you are finished talking with everyone, come back and see me. I'll be interested to see what you've discovered."

With that said, Andrew stood up, smiled, and shook my hand. I was still a little sceptical and unsure whether this would work for me and my organisation. But what did I have to lose? I was intrigued to meet with Gayle and find out more about the importance of emotional intelligence.

I was directed to Gayle's office; her door was open. She was on the phone but beckoned me to come in and take a seat.

As she put the phone down, she smiled and welcomed me. "I believe you've met Andrew," she said. "How do you feel now that you have an understanding of the competencies required to be an emotionally intelligent leader?"

"I'm not sure," I responded. "It all seems a bit confusing and theoretical at the moment. I still have no idea how emotionally intelligent leadership can help my organisation improve."

"I know how you feel," she said. "I felt like that too, when I was sitting in a classroom, learning about emotional intelligence. However, now that I have had the opportunity to utilise what I learnt, it has made a significant impact on how I manage myself and how I lead my team. Let me see if I can help you get a greater feel for what we are doing here."

Gayle continued, "To help you understand the power of emotional intelligence, I want to start with an exercise on the science of emotions."

She handed me a sheet of paper with a table on it.

1. Write down as many feelings as you can recall over the last twenty-four hours.	2. Using the feelings list to help you, write down as many additional feelings as you can recall over the last twenty-four hours.
Total number recalled:	Total number recalled:
Total number of positive:	
Total number of negative:	

"What I'd like you to do is write down as many feelings as you can recall feeling over the last twenty-four hours in the left-hand column," Gayle said. "I'm going to give you sixty seconds. Ready? Go."

I wrote down all the emotions I could remember over the last day.

Gayle interrupted my thoughts. "Okay, time's up. Count up the number of feelings, and write the total number of feelings recalled in the box below."

Embarrassed, I wrote in the number 6.

2. Write down as many feelings as you can recall over the last twenty-four hours.	3. Using the feelings list to help you, write down as many additional feelings as you can recall over the last twenty-four hours.
disappointment happiness worried anger frustration tired	
Total number recalled: 6	Total number recalled:
Total number of positive:	
Total number of negative:	

Gayle then passed me a two-sided sheet that listed all of the feeling words contained in the dictionary. It was quite an extensive list. She gave me time to familiarise myself with the list and then gave me another sixty seconds to recall as many additional feelings I could recall having over the last twenty-four hours, using the sheet as a prompt.

She broke my concentration once more: "Time's up. Now I'd like you to count the total number of feelings recalled this time and write it underneath in the box."

She further explained, "What I then want you to do is reflect on all the feelings across both lists. Specifically, I'd like you count up the number of positive emotions and record this figure, then do the same for the negative emotions."

3. Write down as many feelings you can recall feeling over the last 24 hrs	4. Using the feelings words list to help you, write down as many additional feelings you can recall feeling over the last 24 hrs
disappointment happiness worried anger frustration tired	afraid, manipulated anxious, calm curious, eager disillusioned, concerned irrational, excited, realistic sceptical, relieved
Total number recalled: 6	Total number recalled: 13
Total number of positive: 7	
Total number of negative: 12	

I noted that I was able to recall more emotions using the prompt sheet and had a total of nineteen emotions I could recall feeling, of which seven were positive and the remaining twelve negative. How bad a day was I having?

Gayle continued, "To help us understand the importance and application of emotional intelligence in the workplace, and indeed the activity we just did, I'd like to start by providing some insight gained from recent neuroscientific research. Neuroscience is the study of the biological mechanisms of the brain."

She handed me a diagram, which I looked at with interest.

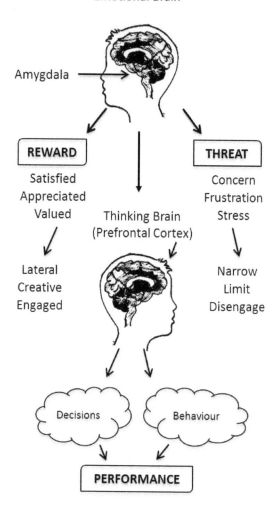

Event

Emotional Brain

Amygdala

REWARD

Satisfied
Appreciated
Valued

Thinking Brain
(Prefrontal Cortex)

THREAT

Concern
Frustration
Stress

Lateral
Creative
Engaged

Narrow
Limit
Disengage

Decisions

Behaviour

PERFORMANCE

Gayle took a deep breath and began, "This research has shown that, whenever an event around us occurs, such as the way someone spoke to us in a meeting, the first thing that happens is our emotional brain, which involves structures such as the amygdala, tags that event as either a reward or a threat. The tag is an emotion; reward emotions are typically positive, and threat emotions are typically negative.

"This emotion tag is communicated to the thinking brain, which involves structures such as the prefrontal cortex. The prefrontal cortex helps us determine good from bad, better from best; it helps us anticipate behaviour and determine our behavioural response to events. As such, the first principle of this program, and indeed one of the underpinnings of emotional intelligence theory, is that the way you feel influences the decisions you make and the behaviour you display.

"Does that make sense?' she asked.

I nodded, and she continued.

"The second interesting finding from research on the neuroscience of emotions is that the emotional tag or emotional signal sent from the emotional brain interacts in a way with the thinking brain that can either enhance or impair its functioning. More specifically, this research has shown that positive emotional tags such as feeling satisfied, valued, or useful tend to enhance the functioning of our prefrontal cortex, helping us think more openly, creatively, and laterally. As such, when we experience positive emotions, either consciously or unconsciously, we tend to be more open to new ideas; we are more engaged and willing to do difficult things and develop new solutions, and we think more deeply about issues and see more options. Positive emotions also increase dopamine levels, which are important for interest in things and learning.

"Conversely," she continued, "this research has shown that negative emotional tags such as feeling concern, worry, frustration, or stress tend to limit the functioning of our prefrontal cortex, narrowing our thinking and limiting our interpretation of events. These negative emotions tend to diminish our cognitive resources. As a result, we become biased in our views; we lose our capacity to evaluate situations objectively and conceptualise our best responses to them. You may have experienced this in a verbal conflict with someone where you felt threatened and thought about all the best or smartest things to say after you walked away from it."

"So putting it simply," I said, "this program shows how to increase reward or positive emotions, and how to decrease or minimise threat emotions, and how to intelligently use emotions to get positive results."

"Exactly," said Gayle. "So when we look at your last twenty-four hours, what does your list suggest?"

"That I have been experiencing more negative emotions than I have positive, but I have not been conscious of these emotions and how they may have impacted my behaviour at work. When I reflect, I do remember feeling frustrated, being short with staff members, and making impulsive decisions, and it's clear now how this could have been seen in my behaviours."

Gayle explained, "Emotional self-awareness is the skill of perceiving and understanding one's own emotions. It is crucial in providing the platform to effectively display productive behaviours associated with the other five competencies. Leaders who display this competency are aware of their feelings, moods, and emotions at work and the causes of these feelings. Sometimes, we are not conscious of the emotion we are feeling, and as a result, we have a limited number of words to describe how we feel in a given situation. We need to expand our emotional vocabulary to identify what we are feeling more accurately. By bringing our subconscious emotions into our conscious brain, we are present with the emotion and understand how it impacts our thoughts, decisions, and behaviours.

"So how do you identify what you are feeling in a given situation?" she asked.

"I'm not sure that I can," I said. "Sometimes, I know I am feeling something but have no idea what it is. I know it is impacting how I am behaving towards others through my tone of voice, facial expressions, and body language, but I often identify that on reflection and after the fact, or only if it is fed back to me. If it is a negative feeling, I tend to gloss over it and hope that it goes away, but it never really does, does it?"

"Not always," Gayle replied, "but hold that thought for later when you explore emotional expression. You are right, though: Our feelings often manifest themselves in our tone of voice, facial expressions, and body language. We tend to embrace our positive emotions and run towards them. With our negative emotions, we often try to hide or dismiss them and rarely determine how they really make us feel. Remember, the way you feel can enhance or impair your decisions and behaviour."

"Your vision will become clear only when you look into your heart. Who looks outside, dreams. Who looks inside, awakens."—Carl Gustav Jung

Take a minute:
Reflect on your emotions
Is your thinking brain enhanced or impaired?
Look at your behaviour.
Did your behaviour impact your performance?

"This is really eye opening," I said. "I can't believe I haven't been aware of this before. I am beginning to realise how disconnected from my emotions I can be and see how this has impacted not only my performance, but how my resultant behaviour has influenced the performance of others in my leadership team."

Gayle smiled and said, "It looks like your emotions are becoming more conscious already. Now we need to understand how to recognise other people's emotions so we can improve the quality of your professional relationships and effectively engage, motivate, and respond to others. Our sales manager, Ricky Scholes, is really good at understanding the emotions of others. I'll give him a call and see if he has some time after lunch to meet with you."

After Gayle arranged my appointment with Ricky, I left her office and went off to lunch. I was already invigorated (a word drawn from the feelings list). I could not believe how unaware I was of my emotions and the way they impacted how effective I was as a leader. As I sat down to eat, I tried to summarise what I had learnt from Gayle so I could focus on what Ricky was going to share with me.

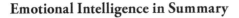
Emotional Intelligence in Summary

> Emotional intelligence involves a set of skills that define how effectively you perceive, understand, reason with, and manage your own and others' feelings.

EI Competency	Definition	Workplace Outcomes
Emotional Self-Awareness	The skill of perceiving and understanding your own emotions.	• The capacity to identify and understand the impact one's own feelings are having on decisions, behaviour, and performance at work • Greater self-awareness

I walked into Ricky's office and was greeted warmly.

"Hi, how are you?" he said enthusiastically. "I believe you've already met with Gayle. You look like you have a lot of things buzzing around your head and are slightly overwhelmed by what you've learnt."

"Yes, you could say that," I replied. "I am still trying to grasp it all. There was quite a lot to take in. Mind you, it's really caught my imagination. I am interested to see how being aware of my own emotions enhances the other competencies in the model."

"Great," said Ricky. "Let me see if I can help you with the second competency, which is emotional awareness of others. Emotional awareness of others is the skill of perceiving and understanding other people's emotions. Leaders who display this competency frequently identify the way people feel about work issues, understand what causes colleagues to feel a certain way, demonstrate an understanding of others' feelings, and make them feel valued."

"This competency seems more obvious to me," I said. "It's about identifying what people are feeling and how it is impacting *their* decisions, behaviour, and performance."

"Yes, that is it, exactly. However, it goes deeper, in that we are trying to understand what causes them to feel certain emotions and show a degree of empathy based on their situation. Is the situation they are in causing the emotional brain to tag the event as a threat (negative emotion) or a reward (positive emotion), and what is then happening to their thinking brain? Is it enhanced or impaired?"

"Wow, that is a real change in my mindset," I responded. "I am often aware of others' emotions but really don't consider how it impacts their ability to perform. I tend to see it from my perspective and how their behaviour is keeping me from achieving what I want to achieve. So regardless of how they feel, I expect them to deliver to my expectation, which shows a degree of insensitivity towards them."

"So how do you accurately recognise the emotions of your team members and colleagues?" Ricky asked.

"I'm not sure," I replied. "I guess a lot is based on intuition; sometimes, I just know when someone is distracted or upset."

"Well, that's all well and good," said Ricky, "but what cues can you look for to confirm those intuitive experiences? How can you tell when someone is stressed or when someone is excited?"

"Oh, I see what you mean. I can often detect changes in their tone of voice. When one of my team members is stressed, she finds it hard to communicate what's on her mind, and her pace is slower; she comes across as nervous. When someone else is excited, he speaks really quickly; his enthusiasm is infectious. In fact, come to think of it, I can always tell when he is disengaged or frustrated purely by the expression on his face and the changes in his body language."

"And how often do you demonstrate that you understand your team's emotions?" he asked.

"Another good question," I replied. "To be honest, I really don't think I do it at all. I believe I am fairly good at recognising the emotions in others, but I rarely acknowledge them; in some instances, I really do not want to deal with them. I guess I dismiss them as not being that important."

"And therein lies the challenge," said Ricky. "We often place our own level of importance on others' emotions and are extremely dismissive in the way we help them handle the situation. This competency is so important to understand, as it enables us to engage with and motivate team members, creating more professional relationships with colleagues. By truly understanding what typically makes people display various emotions in the workplace, we are able to keep them in a reward state and enhance the capacity of their thinking brain, which drives performance.

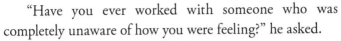

"Have you ever worked with someone who was completely unaware of how you were feeling?" he asked.

"I can think of a few, Ricky."

"So how did it make you feel?" he asked, smiling.

I thought for a moment and responded, "I hated working there. I felt unappreciated. I was disengaged. I had no motivation. The organisational environment was toxic; everyone was in it for themselves. Politics and backstabbing seem to be the norm. This caused high staff turnover, high absenteeism, and increased levels of conflict, leading to numerous cases of bullying. No one seemed to care."

Ricky nodded. "I can see your emotionally vocabulary has already begun to grow," he said. "It seems so obvious, but when we are under pressure or stressed, we tend to display emotionally unintelligent behaviours more frequently and completely forget the impact our behaviour can have on others. Sometimes, we need to take a step back and see the situation from the perspective of others and demonstrate empathy and understanding."

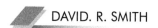
"I've learned that people will forget what you said, people will forget what you did, but people will never forget how you made them feel."—Maya Angelou

"You're so right, Ricky," I said. "I've become so immersed in my own world that I neglected my responsibility towards understanding others. Because I have not been aware of my own emotions, I have had limited capacity to understand what causes emotions in others; as such, I have most likely contributed to my leadership team being in a threat state."

Ricky laughed and said, "Well, it looks like it is all making sense. If we aren't aware of our own emotions, how can we understand the emotions of others? And when we put colleagues or subordinates in a threat state, relating back to Andrew's simple success formula, they do not perform the physical or mental aspects of their role as their emotions impair the ability of their thinking brain. That's why being aware of the emotions of others is crucial for creating engaged, motivated teams and leaders.

"Did Gayle talk about the SCARF model?" Ricky asked.

"No, she didn't mention that," I said.

"One of the best starting places for improving both self-awareness and awareness of others," he explained "is feelings. Feelings follow logical patterns. Our capacity to identify and understand emotions is possible because these patterns exist. We are happy when we achieve something and disappointed when we don't.

"Recent insights gleaned from social neuroscience have identified five categories of events that can activate positive or negative emotions in our interactions with others. These five categories were recently conceptualised by author David Rock as a model to help people collaborate with others. By understanding SCARF, we can intelligently demonstrate behaviours associated with the five categories to help us resolve conflicts or collaborate effectively with others."

"So what does SCARF stand for?" I asked.

Ricky stood up and wrote the following on a flip chart:

S – Status
C – Certainty
A – Autonomy
R – Relatedness
F – Fairness

Ricky continued, "**Status** is about relative importance to others. Where do I sit in the pecking order in relation to others? It can be incredibly easy to unknowingly threaten someone's status, simply by providing advice or giving feedback.

"**Certainty** concerns being able to predict the future," he went on. "Any kind of significant change creates uncertainty, so we need to ensure that we have clearly delineated plans that accurately articulate desirable outcomes and expectations."

"**Autonomy** provides a sense of control over one's environment," he said. "It is about having the ability to choose. Micro-management, for example, can generate a strong threat response, which causes people to become disengaged.

"**Relatedness** is a sense of safety with others: friend or foe. It is about affiliation and creating social connections. Am I part of the group, or am I considered an outsider?

"And **fairness** is a perception of fair exchanges between people," he concluded. "Are we managing people consistently? Are the ground rules clear? Are we remunerated in an equitable way? Clear expectations, transparency, and increased communication can help ensure that fair exchanges occur."

Ricky paused and then continued, "If you remember back to the model Gayle shared with you on the neuroscience of emotions, these five categories activate the reward or threat state in the brain. For example, if people feel their status is being challenged, their emotional brain tags the event as a threat using similar brain networks that respond to a threat to their life. In the same way, if they have been recognised for their contribution and perceive an increase in fairness, the emotional brain tags the event as a reward, using the same reward circuitry as receiving a monetary reward."

"I can see how understanding these five categories could help me and my organisation function more effectively," I replied thoughtfully. "It is a really great framework for developing my own self-awareness, the awareness of others, and the key triggers that can cause a threat or reward state that will influence thoughts and behaviours."

"It certainly helps explain why people react differently to different situations," he said. "If we can modify our behaviour to proactively enhance how we respond to events at work or colleagues, we reduce conflict and begin to work more collaboratively with each other."

"And I guess if we are aware of our emotions and have a greater understanding of others' emotions, we will be more equipped to express how we are feeling in an appropriate way?" I asked.

"Absolutely," he replied quickly. "And as you now know, the next competency in the model is that of authenticity. I'm going to leave that to Jennifer Vidic in marketing. She is much better at expressing herself than I am. My advice, though, would be to come back tomorrow. You're looking a bit tired; I think your brain needs some time to refresh so you can fully understand the remaining five competencies. Give her a call on your way home on this number. According to her calendar, she's free tomorrow morning."

I left the office, and as Ricky noted, I was a little tired. It had been a most interesting day, and I had a gut feeling that tomorrow was going to be just as good, if not better.

The next day, feeling refreshed from a good night's sleep, I returned to the premises and asked for Jennifer at reception. I was informed she was running ten minutes late. I opened my notepad and used the time to update my summary.

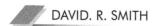

DAVID. R. SMITH

Emotional Intelligence in Summary

Emotional intelligence involves a set of skills that define how effectively you perceive, understand, reason with, and manage your own and others' feelings.		
EI Competency	**Definition**	**Workplace Outcomes**
Emotional Self-Awareness	The skill of perceiving and understanding your own emotions.	• The capacity to identify and understand the impact one's own feelings are having on decisions, behaviour, and performance at work • Greater self-awareness
Emotional Awareness of Others	The skill of perceiving and understanding others' emotions.	• Greater understanding of others and how to engage, respond, motivate, and connect with them • Interpersonal effectiveness • Understand SCARF triggers

40

Jennifer seemed to be a bit frazzled on her arrival at reception and was most apologetic for the delay. It was a beautiful day, so she suggested we go and sit on the bench outside, as she needed a change of environment.

"I believe you already met with Gayle and Ricky?" she asked.

"Yes, I did," I replied. "It was most informative. I was amazed how disconnected I was from my emotions and the impact it could have on my own behaviours and the behaviours of others."

"Yes," she said, nodding. "As I hope you have learnt, self-awareness is vitally important and helps you improve on some of the other competencies, one of which is authenticity. Any idea what we mean by authenticity?"

"From memory of my conversation with Andrew, I believe it is the ability to effectively express your own emotions and being seen as trustworthy."

"Spot on." She went on to explain, "Authenticity is about how openly and effectively you express how you feel, how appropriately you express specific emotions, how frequently you provide positive feedback to colleagues, and how consistently you honour commitments.

"Most importantly, though, it's about how frequently you express your emotions at the right time, to the right degree, to the right person, and in the right place."

"Authenticity is the alignment of head, mouth, heart, and feet—thinking, saying, feeling, and doing the same thing—consistently. This builds trust. Followers love leaders they can trust."—Lance Secretan

"How would you describe your level of openness in the workplace?" Jennifer asked.

"That's a tough question," I replied. "I do find it hard to express myself. I've always been taught to keep my emotions in and not let them show."

Jennifer smiled and said, "I think this is one of the hardest of the six competencies to live, simply because not everyone is wired to share how people make them feel. It is a trust thing. It takes time to build trusting relationships, especially when we are under the impression that showing emotions is a sign of weakness. However, we tend to express our positive emotions more openly than we would our negative ones. This may because we don't want to fall out with someone we work closely with. It may also be that we work in an environment where we may be ridiculed for expressing our opinion, so we bottle feelings up.

"Let me try and give you an example," she said. "Imagine you and I were in a meeting with the leadership team, consisting of your peers and your manager. On each occasion when you try to contribute to the meeting, I jump in and talk over you. There are a number of ways you could handle this situation. Firstly, you could do nothing. You may then leave the meeting, go home, and vent to a partner or close friend regarding what transpired at the meeting to get it off your chest. However, is that the right time, the right degree, the right person, and the right place?"

"No, it is not," I replied.

"So what do you think might happen at the next meeting?" she asked.

"You'll do the same again," I said.

"Exactly, and if I continue to interrupt you at future meetings?" she asked.

"Well, eventually I am likely to get annoyed and lose my temper and have a go at you," I said.

"Yes, that may well happen. But would you consider yourself to be expressing your emotions at the right time, to the right degree, to the right person, and in the right place?" she asked again.

"Well, it's certainly the right person," I replied, "but I can see what you are saying. It may not be the right time for this conversation; if I am getting annoyed, it is most likely not going to be in the right degree, and the meeting is certainly not the appropriate place to have a conversation with you. And I am likely to come out as the bad guy, as I have attacked you."

"Which leads us to a third alternative: using feeling statements," she suggested. "We go back to self-awareness and using our emotional vocabulary, identify how you feel when I interrupt you and talk over you. Let's assume that you feel I am not valuing your opinion, so therefore I am disrespecting you. After the meeting, you could pull me to one side in an appropriate place and say, 'Jennifer, I feel disrespected in these meetings when you constantly interrupt and talk over me because you don't seem to appreciate my contribution. In future, I would like you to give me the opportunity to share my views, as I feel I have something valuable to contribute to the team.'"

Jennifer continued, "Using feeling statements removes the accusatory tone we sometimes use and therefore reduces the likelihood of getting a defensive reaction from others as it is less confrontational."

"I can think of many instances when I have witnessed people expressing how they feel in the wrong place, at the wrong time, in the wrong degree, and to the wrong people," I said. "I also recall when I have expressed myself in an inappropriate manner. On reflection, I can see where ineffective expression has caused staff to go into a threat state and simply shut down, or explode."

"If you are guarded and don't express how you feel about work issues, it takes longer to build trust and develop genuine relationships," said Jennifer. "Being guarded results in false assumptions and mistrust. We need improve our ability to give information back to others in an emotionally intelligent way, to help change their behaviours. If you recall from that meeting scenario, if you don't express your feedback, nothing happens or you are seen to be the one behaving poorly, if you express your feedback without any regard for the time, place, or person. Being blunt can result in a flight-or-fight response."

"We can also be more authentic and build more trusting relationships by disclosing information to others," she explained. "You may not like presenting to large groups on short notice, as it makes you feel anxious if you don't have time to prepare. If you don't share this information, your manager may not realise how it makes you feel each time he asks you to present at a meeting."

"Especially if he has no emotional awareness of others," I said, laughing.

"And yet so true. Effective emotional expression involves consideration of the time, place, context, and other party. It involves being open and authentic with your thoughts and feelings but in a way that is mindful of these other factors."

"Even at this early stage of understanding," I said, "it appears to me that all the competencies are interlinked. If you are not aware of your own emotions and not able to identify how you are really feeling, you are likely to express yourself in an emotionally unintelligent manner, that is, at the wrong time, to the wrong degree, in the wrong place, and to the wrong person. Added to that, if you are not demonstrating that you are aware of others' emotions and are not empathetic towards them, team members are less likely to disclose information on what makes them feel anxious, stressed, or excited."

"And we also need to be mindful that leaders need to focus on catching people doing things right," Jennifer added. "Authenticity includes how effective we are at providing positive feedback to people so that they perform to expectation. We are programmed to identify problems and threats, and thus we tend to overlook what we are doing well and miss the opportunity to celebrate success.

"Which would you prefer to experience," she asked rhetorically: "the emotions associated with success or the emotions associated with failure?"

"I can also see how authenticity can impact the five drivers in the SCARF model and how easily the language we use can put people in a threat or reward state," I replied.

"In relation to our simple success formula—physical, mental, emotional—when we express ourselves effectively, we enhance our mental capability and are able to deliver high-quality outcomes, both internally to numerous stakeholders and externally to our customers. By being authentic," Jennifer said, "we develop more trusting relationships and through higher levels of engagement improve performance."

"Always remember," she concluded, "people will detect your feelings no matter how good you think you are at disguising them. Whether you know it or not, it is displayed in your tone of voice, your body language, and your facial expressions. If your emotional expression is poor, people may make incorrect assumptions about the nature and cause of your feelings and subsequent behaviours. People start to make stuff up. We certainly don't need that to be happening when we are in the process of making an important decision. But I'll leave that to Maxwell Hughes, our finance manager, who I believe is next on your list to talk about emotional reasoning."

"That's great, Jennifer. I must say I am feeling a lot less sceptical than when I first arrived here. Your organisation seems so passionate about what you've learnt and the impact it is having. The more I hear, the more I believe. So far, I am tagging this event as a positive emotion and feeling quite excited."

"Good for you," replied Jennifer.

And with that said, I left the marketing department and headed off for my meeting with Maxwell in finance.

DAVID. R. SMITH

Emotional Intelligence in Summary

Emotional intelligence involves a set of skills that define how effectively you perceive, understand, reason with and manage your own and others' feelings.		
EI Competency	**Definition**	**Workplace Outcomes**
Emotional Self-Awareness	The skill of perceiving and understanding your own emotions.	• The capacity to identify and understand the impact one's own feelings are having on decisions, behaviour, and performance at work • Greater self-awareness
Emotional Awareness of Others	The skill of perceiving and understanding others' emotions.	• Greater understanding of others and how to engage, respond, motivate, and connect with them • Interpersonal effectiveness • Understand SCARF triggers
Authenticity	The skill of expressing your own emotions effectively.	• Creating greater understanding amongst colleagues about yourself • Creating trust and perceptions of genuineness amongst colleagues

The finance department was a lot quieter than both the sales and the marketing department. Team members were all immersed in their computer screens. Maxwell's office was at the far end of the room; he saw me approaching and waved for me to come and join him.

"Hi Maxwell," I said. "Thanks for agreeing to meet with me."

"Easiest decision I had to make all day," he replied. "We all believe in sharing what we have learnt, well, except with a direct competitor, of course. So what brings you here?"

"I run a really good organisation, but I want it to be great. I just happened to stumble across the article about your CEO and felt like emotional intelligence could be the missing ingredient to help me achieve that goal. I've invested in a number of leadership programs, with limited impact. So I did some research on the Internet, decided to give it a go, and called your CEO to have a chat. He suggested that I come and talk to him and some of his staff, and I am very glad I did."

"Well, that's great," replied Maxwell. "Any idea what emotional reasoning entails?"

"Off the top of my head, I believe it has to do with effective decision-making."

"It certainly does, but it goes a little deeper than just making decisions," he explained. "Emotional reasoning is using emotional information from yourself and others, when reasoning, planning, and making decisions. It is about considering your own feelings when making decisions, demonstrating to others that you have considered their feelings, and once the decision has been made, effectively communicating that decision to gain stakeholder commitment."

"So it could be a really important competency for managing change in organisations?" I asked.

"Yes, it can be. I've subsequently come across a few change managers who struggle, as they are insensitive towards other people's feelings and often fail to notice how the process of change makes people feel. That puts employees into a threat state, which creates barriers, and there is less buy-in from staff. The thinking brain's capacity is narrowed, as they don't feel listened to. When they communicate a decision, they use inappropriate channels of communication, which once again creates a threat state environment, causing less buy-in from the stakeholders," he concluded.

"So," Maxwell asked, "how conscious are you of your feelings and the feelings of others when you make decisions?"

"I guess it depends on the situation," I replied. "I know in the past, I used to make a number of decisions based on gut feel, but less so now. I think that is partly due to the fact that the decisions I make are more significant. So as a result, I take more time to analyse the data to make sure it correlates with my initial thoughts."

"Excellent. And in its simplest form, that is what emotional reasoning is all about. What we know is that we have two sources of data: emotional data and technical data. What we need to do is use both emotional data and technical data to make an expansive decision, rather than limiting ourselves to one or the other."

"We know too much and feel too little of those emotions from which a good life springs."—Bertrand Russell

"People have differing abilities in displaying this competency," Maxwell continued. "If you are a process-oriented person or left brain dominant, you tend to favour the technical aspects of decision-making. Look at me. I'm an accountant. Alternatively, if you are people-oriented or right brain dominant, you tend to listen to your emotions and make more impulsive decisions based on gut feel. Think of Ricky, our sales manager. Neither methodology is wrong. However, if you use both sources of data, you are likely to get a more innovative or creative solution.

"As an accountant, that knowledge was challenging in how I made decisions," he said, laughing out loud. "But I can see now how important it is to utilise emotional data to make more effective decisions and, importantly for me, in how I then communicate that decision."

"I can see now why people in sales often clash with the finance department," I said. "They work so differently and have different perspectives and priorities."

"Yes, that's a very good point," he replied. "People's personality styles do impact how competent they are at displaying emotionally intelligent behaviours; we have used DiSC—you know, 'Dominant, Influence, Steadiness and Conscientiousness'—to help our employees become more aware of themselves and understand how their style impacts their working relationships and their ability to display emotional intelligence, but that's a whole other story.

"Let me share an example with you," he said.

Maxwell handed me a sheet of paper with an excerpt from *Blink*, a book by Malcolm Gladwell. It read as follows:

"The world of classical music—particularly in its European home—was until very recently the preserve of white men. But over the past few decades, the classical music world has undergone a revolution. Many musicians thought that conductors were abusing their power and playing favourites. They wanted the audition process to be formalised, therefore, musicians were identified not by name but by number.

Screens were erected between the committee and the musicians, and if the person auditioning cleared his or her throat or made any kind of identifiable sound, they were ushered out and given a new number. And as these new rules were put in place around the country, an extraordinary thing happened: orchestras began to hire women.

Gladwell ties this extraordinary story into the overall theme of *Blink* by explaining that our first impression of how players sound is often corrupted by how they look. In this case, it compromises the ability of even highly trained musicians to make split-second evaluations of a player's skill.

What the classical music world realised was that what they thought was a pure and powerful first impression—listening to someone play—was in fact hopelessly corrupted.

Some people look like they play better than they actually sound, because they look confident and have good posture, one musician, a veteran of many auditions, said. Other people look awful when they play but sound great. Other people have that belaboured look when they play, but you can't hear it in the sound. There is always this dissonance between what you see and hear. The audition begins the first second the person is in view.

The chapter goes on to quote none other than Julie

Landsman, recently retired principal French horn player for the Metropolitan Opera in New York, who says that she's found herself distracted by the position of someone's mouth.

If they put their mouthpiece up in an unusual position, you might immediately think, Oh my, it can't possibly work. There are so many possibilities. Some horn players use a brass instrument, and some use nickel-silver, and the kind of horn the person is playing tells you something about what city they come from, their teacher, and their school, and that pedigree is something that influences your opinion.

I've been in auditions without screens, and I can assure you that I was prejudiced. I began to listen with my eyes, and there is no way that your eyes don't affect your judgment. The only true way to listen is with your ears and your heart.

Gladwell closes this chapter by noting that screens allowed audition committees to form more accurate impressions of players, without being prejudiced by their appearance.

Until they listened to her with just their ears, however, they had no idea she was so good. When the screen created a pure Blink moment, a small miracle happened, the kind of small miracle that is always possible when we take charge of the first two seconds: they saw her for who she truly was."

"Thoughts?" Maxwell enquired.

"What a fascinating example," I said. "It shows how they were making decisions based on limited data, relying on technical information and not listening with their heart. Understanding emotional data provides us with the opportunity to use our emotions to make an expansive decision by listening, so we don't prejudge situations or display an unconscious bias. I guess that's why 'The Voice' created such a buzz, as it gave judges the opportunity to listen to a singer and make a decision based on what they heard rather than what they saw."

"Yes, I have watched some of 'The Voice' too, and it does highlight the discrepancies that can occur if you only rely on one source of data. I'm interested: How often are your head and heart in sync with each other when you make decisions?" asked Maxwell.

Based on what I've learnt, not very often," I replied. "I can see how understanding what I am feeling can help me make more effective decisions. When I am stressed or anxious, I tend to default to the technical data and over-analyse, as my brain does not have the capacity to reason and make the decision. I lose the confidence to make decisions based on those feelings. However, when I am excited or feeling optimistic, I tend to make a number of decisions based on gut feel, some of which come back to haunt me. It tends to be either one or the other, but very rarely is it both in congruence.

"I can remember a time a few years ago, when my manager wanted to dismiss one of my state managers. In his eyes, this person was not performing, and being a very emotional leader, he was basing his decision purely on emotion and limited technical information. When you analysed the data, it was apparent that the revenue was being generated in line with agreed targets, yet it was not translating into the P and L. There was an accounting issue. However, he was adamant that this was not the case and was putting pressure on me to terminate the employee. Interestingly, my gut was telling me no, this was not right. And on reflection now, with my exposure to the SCARF model, I can see how this created a negative tag for me, as I did not view this event as fair."

"And what happened?" Maxwell asked.

"In the end, I left the organisation, as the decision to terminate my state manager was compromising my values; my head and heart were in sync. I used emotional data. It simply did not feel right. I used technical data: The financial

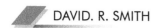

information gathered was incorrect; it was not logical. I no longer wanted to be a part of that process."

"And decision-making is very much situational," Maxwell responded. "When we buy a house, we often defer to emotional information. We visualise living in the house and identify how it would make us feel. We get butterflies in our stomach and get very excited. However, if we fail to research the area or complete a survey on the house, we may end up in a flood plain or have structural issues."

He continued, "Alternatively, when an organisation is required to make staff cuts to reduce the bottom line, a financial controller is likely to use purely technical data by looking at the numbers. Look at the minimal impact and get rid of the most expensive person in the department. However, they do not identify the emotional impact on others that this person leaving may have in that department. They could be the glue that holds the team together; their subsequent dismissal may have greater impact in terms of morale and subsequent motivation."

"So when we make decisions," I suggested, "we need to be in touch with our own emotions, understand how our own feelings are impacting the decision, and combine this with facts and information. We also need to be mindful of how the decision being made impacts how others feel and ensure we express the decision in an appropriate manner to the relevant stakeholders."

"Looks like you have come a long way in the last twenty-four hours," Maxwell said. "The next step is to learn how to manage and control those emotions so you can make more effective decisions and increase the frequency of expressing yourself in the right time, to the right degree, to the right person, and in the right place."

"With each competency, it makes more sense," I replied. "My gut feeling tells me that I have taken up enough of your time, and looking at the clock, it is nearly 2:00 p.m. I am expected in HR to catch up with Hazel at 2:15. This expansive decision-making is easy, isn't it, Maxwell?"

Maxwell smiled, stood up, and shook my hand. Once again, I did a quick update of what I had learnt from Maxwell and added it to my summary.

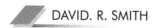

Emotional Intelligence in Summary

Emotional intelligence involves a set of skills that define how effectively you perceive, understand, reason with, and manage your own and others' feelings.		
EI Competency	**Definition**	**Workplace Outcomes**
Emotional Self-Awareness	The skill of perceiving and understanding your own emotions.	• The capacity to identify and understand the impact one's own feelings are having on decisions, behaviour, and performance at work • Greater self-awareness
Emotional Awareness of Others	The skill of perceiving and understanding others' emotions.	• Greater understanding of others and how to engage, respond, motivate, and connect with them • Interpersonal effectiveness • Understand SCARF triggers
Authenticity	The skill of expressing your own emotions effectively.	• Creating greater understanding amongst colleagues about yourself • Creating trust and perceptions of genuineness amongst colleagues
Emotional Reasoning	The skill of utilising emotional information in decision-making.	• Enhanced decision making, where different types of information are gathered and processed • Greater buy-in from others into decisions that are made

When I arrived for my appointment with Hazel Keane, she was in a meeting with an employee. I took a seat and waited. After ten minutes, her door opened, and she walked the employee out of the office. When she returned, she appeared to be a bit frustrated with the previous meeting's deliberations and explained she needed a couple of minutes to tie up a few loose ends.

When she came out, she suggested that we go and grab a drink from the staff meeting area, which turned out to be a bright, cheery space with a broad array of seating options, including beanbags, egg chairs, and designer couches. Thankfully, she didn't choose the bean bags; Hazel led me to a booth overlooking the park. It was quite a beautiful view to behold.

"Thanks for your patience," Hazel said. "It's been one of those days." She looked out of the window and smiled. "I love this view," she said. "It reminds me of the outdoors: a place where I always feel relaxed and at peace. I often come here to refresh during the throes of a hectic day."

"It sounds like your job can be fairly stressful," I asked.

"Dealing with people always is," she replied. "There are always challenges. At the same time, though, it can be rewarding to see our employees develop, succeed, and grow as people. I take great pride in that. Plus, I have learnt how important it is to manage and control my emotions, which is of course why you are sitting in front of me."

"Yes, indeed I am," I replied. "I think this is one area where I could probably improve considerably. I can think of a few occasions when my emotions got the better of me."

"As I explain to everyone," she began, "and I'm sure you've heard before, it is impossible to behave with emotional intelligence every single minute of the day. There are always going to be occasions when we feel overwhelmed by a situation that causes us to react in an inappropriate manner. As such, emotional self-management is how effectively you manage your own emotions. It involves engaging in activities that make you feel positive at work, exploring the causes of workplace events that upset you, and then developing the capability to move on from upsetting events."

Hazel continued, "In today's business world of increased demands, multitasking, and higher levels of general stress, our ability to create positive moods in ourselves—to be optimistic and resilient in the face of difficulty, to see opportunities in situations rather than consequences, and to manage our strong emotions in an appropriate manner—creates good energy. And this good energy radiates from us and has a positive impact on everyone we interact with at work every day.

"Can you think about a time when you came to work with a strong feeling? What impact did that have on your decisions, your behaviour, or your performance?" she asked.

"Yes, I can," I responded. "A couple of weeks ago, I was reviewing the end-of-year results. We were doing really well, but we could be doing better, and I was frustrated with the situation. I spent most of the night tossing and turning. I had all these thoughts going through my head. What could I be doing differently? Why weren't we excelling? I got a lousy night's sleep. When I left for work the next morning, I was in a terrible mood. My brain felt all fuzzy. As a result, when I walked into the office, I was very short with the receptionist. In the morning meeting with my leadership team, I was very blunt and had limited tolerance for their comments; I became quite sarcastic. I found it hard to think straight and remember simple stuff. I also remember having a limited attention span and procrastinated over what I would normally consider straightforward decisions. It was awful."

"It's amazing how our emotions can have such a significant impact on our decisions, thoughts, and behaviour," Hazel said. "We need to explore the causes of things that upset us at work and develop strategies that enable us to move on from them. It all links back to the science of emotions and the relationship between our emotional brain, which encompasses the amygdala, and our thinking brain, which houses the prefrontal cortex. Do you remember talking with Gayle about this relationship?"

"Yes, I do," I said eagerly. "Let me have a go at recalling it. Whenever an event around us occurs, the first thing that happens is our emotional brain tags the event as either a reward or a threat. The tag is an emotion; reward emotions are typically positive, and threat emotions are typically negative."

"Very good," Hazel noted.

I continued, "This emotional tag is communicated to the prefrontal cortex. If the tag is positive, the functioning of the brain is enhanced; if it is a negative tag, the functioning of the brain is impaired."

"And in which scenario do you think we display the unproductive leadership state?" asked Hazel.

"When the prefrontal cortex receives a negative communication and is subsequently impaired," I replied.

"Exactly," said Hazel. "Let me show you a diagram to explain."

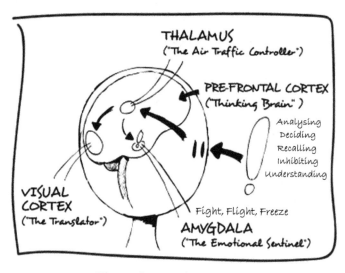

THALAMUS
("The Air Traffic Controller")

PRE-FRONTAL CORTEX
("Thinking Brain")

Analysing
Deciding
Recalling
Inhibiting
Understanding

VISUAL
CORTEX
("The Translator")

Fight, Flight, Freeze
AMYGDALA
("The Emotional Sentinel")

Physical Mental Emotional

"Our prefrontal cortex," Hazel continued, "is designed to think, analyse, understand, make decisions, recall information, and create inhibitions. Unfortunately, the prefrontal cortex is an exhaustible resource and runs out of energy over the course of the day. When we experience strong emotions, survival mechanisms can start operating that limit the effectiveness of our prefrontal cortex. When our thinking brain is hijacked, oxygen is diminished and used to create survival behaviours: flight, fight, or freeze. The term 'amygdala hijack' comes from this experience. This is why, when we are very tired, frustrated, annoyed, fearful, or angry, we don't always think clearly and we react to situations in a way that we later regret. Does that make sense?"

"It certainly does, Hazel. Now I understand why road rage happens. We are experiencing an amygdala hijack."

"Correct," said Hazel. "So the key to managing our emotions is in our ability to build our resilience so we are less likely to experience the amygdala hijack, which makes it hard to think, analyse, understand, recall information, or create inhibitions. If we manage our emotions more effectively, our stress levels decrease, so we don't lose our temper as often, we remain focused, and we refrain from making impulsive decisions that prove to be costly in the future."

"I'm sure there have been occasions when you needed to calm down at work or felt overwhelmed with the demands placed upon you," she said. "How did you manage this?"

"When I feel like I am about to lose my temper, I tend to walk away so I remove myself from the situation; I take a deep breath and count to ten. I can now link this action to emotional expression. I want to express my emotion at the right time, to the right degree, to the right person, and in the right place, rather than react impulsively."

"When I am stressed or overwhelmed by work pressures," I continued, "I make a list of my deliverables and then prioritise them in order of importance. Sometimes, I go for a walk to get some fresh air; I may ring my partner and have a chat with them. Each of these things helps to change my mindset and get back on track."

"What we are trying to do is implement strategies to increase the thinking brain's capacity to operate more efficiently and for longer periods of time," added Hazel. "The most effective way to do this (but often the hardest) is to get more sleep, which helps explain your behaviour in the example you shared earlier. If we don't sleep long enough, we do not enter into deep sleep, so when we awake, our brain still feels frazzled, as it did not have the chance to refresh. Its capacity is limited. As we go through the day, we find it hard to recall simple facts, get frustrated, and often take it out on others. The next best thing to sleep is meditation, which provides you with the opportunity to relax and reflect on situations, which helps stimulate and reprogram your thinking brain. You can also exercise more, eat more healthily, regulate your breathing, change your environment by going for a walk, or talk to someone you have a close relationships with to vent your emotions. All these strategies are designed to re-engage your thinking brain so you can display the productive leadership being states more frequently."

"When we can no longer change a situation, we are challenged to change ourselves."—Viktor Frankl

Hazel carried on, "In Steven Covey's book *The 7 Habits of Highly Effective People*, the first habit is being proactive: I am free to choose and am responsible for my choices. When we fail to manage our emotions, we are a product of our circumstances and become ineffective and perceived as temperamental. However, when we build resilience, we develop the freedom to choose our response to any stimulus or event by examining our own thoughts, moods, and behaviours before we react."

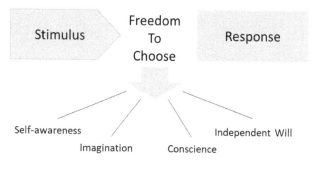

Stimulus Response Diagram

"This is where emotional self-control ties in. Emotional self-control is how effectively you regulate the emotions you experience. Specifically, how frequently you can remain focussed when stressed or anxious, demonstrate anger appropriately, control your temper, and not become impulsive under stress. There is an intrinsic part of self-management: If you can't manage your emotions, how can you control them?"

"Relating this to our simple success formula—physical, mental, emotional—when we fail to manage and control our emotions," she explained, "our mental capacity is diminished, as the thinking brain is impaired; we can't think, understand, or recall information, and we do not put in the hard work. As a result, quality and productivity decline."

"How conscious are you of your reactions or behaviours when you are stressed or under pressure?" Hazel asked me.

"The answer to that is clear: not very often," I replied candidly. "I tend to be aware after the event and when I reflect on conversations I had. I remember one time when I had to choose between two candidates for a role. I was so flustered, I could not make the decision, and yet there was a clear standout candidate. I can also remember incidents when I have been extremely sarcastic to attendees at meetings for no apparent reason; my actions seemed to happen before I realised it. However, I can see now that this was linked to the SCARF triggers. I had just completed a major piece of work and did not feel I had received the recognition I deserved. There was no appreciation for the hard work I put in. I guess that's why I behaved in that manner."

"And that is where self-control differs from self-management," Hazel added. "Self-control focuses on your threshold for coping with strong emotions. When we feel the building of pressure, we experience the amygdala hijack and become extremely reactive to events or situations. This then manifests itself in how we react to things that upset us; we lose patience when things don't go as planned. If our thinking capacity is impaired, this reaction will be worse, and our behaviours will be from a position of anger, and we are unable to control our temper."

She continued, "What we need to do is ensure we are managing our emotions so that we are able to control our reactions to those emotions. We often believe we have managed our emotions related to certain events; however, if we haven't explored what upset us, we rarely move on from the event that triggered the emotion. If we don't express how we feel to the right person, to the right degree, at the right time, there is a strong likelihood that our reaction to a past event will raise its ugly head in a nonrelated encounter.

"In your example, you felt unappreciated; if you did not express how you feel, you may very well react and attack someone for no apparent reason. We also get this surge of adrenaline when people compromise our values. If we think back to that meeting scenario when I talk over you, if you value respect, you are more likely to react to that situation in an inappropriate manner."

"I can see the link to values, Hazel," I responded. "I can remember numerous occasions when people, often teachers, made assumptions about my children or chastised them. I felt the pressure gauge rising, and before I knew it, I had reacted with some inappropriate comment in my child's defence."

"And as long as you are aware," Hazel replied, "you can reflect and create a strategy to better manage the emotion in the future. And in doing so, you will have more effective relationships in the workplace because once you understand yourself, you have increased your capacity to become more aware of those around you and then be in a better position to influence their moods and emotions too."

"I'm really glad we had this conversation," I said. "This has clarified in my mind how interrelated the competencies are, in addition to their individual importance. I've had a light bulb moment. I'm really looking forward to catching up with Andrew again to share with him what I've learned over the last couple of days."

"That's great," Hazel responded. "Andrew prides himself

on developing a positive mood, remaining calm under pressure, and reacting to frustrations in a measured and thoughtful manner. He has a certain charisma, an infectious positive energy that we all like to be around. And in so doing, he brings out positive emotions and moods in our leadership team. I'm sure this final part of your journey will provide you with the catalyst to inspire your team to greatness.

Before I headed towards my final meeting with Andrew, I took a few minutes to prepare and summarise what I had learned so far in my game plan. I wanted to make sure that my thinking brain was refreshed so I could focus on the final piece of the jigsaw puzzle: inspiring performance in others.

Emotional Intelligence in Summary

Emotional intelligence involves a set of skills that define how effectively you perceive, understand, reason with, and manage your own and others' feelings.		
EI Competency	**Definition**	**Workplace Outcomes**
Emotional Self-Awareness	The skill of perceiving and understanding your own emotions.	• The capacity to identify and understand the impact one's own feelings are having on decisions, behaviour, and performance at work • Greater self-awareness
Emotional Awareness of Others	The skill of perceiving and understanding others' emotions.	• Greater understanding of others and how to engage, respond, motivate, and connect with them • Interpersonal effectiveness • Understand SCARF triggers
Emotional Expression	The skill of expressing your own emotions effectively.	• Creating greater understanding amongst colleagues about yourself • Creating trust and perceptions of genuineness amongst colleagues
Emotional Reasoning	The skill of utilising emotional information in decision-making.	• Enhanced decision making where different types of information are gathered and processed • Greater buy-in from others into decisions that are made.

Emotional Self-Management	The skill of effectively managing and controlling your own emotions.	• Improved job satisfaction and engagement • Improved ability to cope with high work demands • Enhanced productivity and performance • Improved emotional well-being • The capacity to think clearly in stressful situations • The capacity to effectively deal with situations that cause strong emotions

I walked in to Andrew's office for the second time. I was feeling very excited. This was the final conversation: How could emotional intelligence help me to inspire my team to greatness?

"Welcome," boomed Andrew. "Come in. Sit down. I'm a little bit under the pump but have scheduled thirty minutes where you have my undivided attention. I've been hearing good feedback from my team; they feel you are getting a great deal out of the experience and are beginning to grasp the concept of emotional intelligence and how it applies to leadership. But I'm interested to hear what you identified as the big takeaways so far."

Well, this was quite a daunting prospect. My heart was racing. I took a deep breath and began.

"Well, Andrew," I said, "I must admit I was a little sceptical when I contacted you. I was not sure whether emotional intelligence was going to work for me, but I am pleased to say, having spent time with your team, I have a greater appreciation and understanding for emotional intelligence and how it applies to leadership.

"Here's what I now know," I continued. "Emotional intelligence is a set of skills that help you perceive, understand, reason with, express, and manage the emotions of yourself and others. It has been obvious to me that I was not conscious of how my emotions were impacting my decisions, behaviours, and performance, and how this impacted the behaviours of those I interact with. The key is being self-aware. I need to be present with the role feelings are playing in how I operate in a leadership capacity."

"That is so important to remember," Andrew interjected. "Self-awareness is the foundation for developing all of the leadership competencies of EI; awareness of your own emotions will help you to be more expressive, reason better, and manage your emotions more effectively. Let me explain: If you are not aware of your emotions, you will find it hard to manage these emotions. If you are not managing your emotions, you will be less likely to control these emotions. If you are emotionally out of control, your ability to express how you feel effectively at the right time, to the right degree, to the right person, and in the right place will be diminished. You will also find it hard to remain focused at work and will feel pressured into making impulsive decisions; you will experience increased incidences of the amygdala hijack. As your thinking brain capacity is impaired and narrowed, you may be seen as temperamental, reactive to situations, guarded, and untrustworthy; your decision-making capability will be questioned."

"That's a really great and succinct way of looking at it," I responded. "By having that greater understanding of myself, it gives me increased capacity to be aware of and acknowledge the emotions of others, so I am more equipped to manage their emotions and thus facilitate high performance."

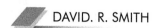
"What is necessary to change a person is to change his awareness of himself."—Abraham Maslow

"Exactly," replied Andrew. "The more we are aware of our own emotions and subsequent behaviours, the more capable we are of identifying and managing the emotions of other. We utilise the strategies we have developed successfully for ourselves and share with others we manage, so they become more self-aware and build their capacity to manage their emotions and their subsequent behaviour."

He continued, "Have you ever worked with someone who walked around the office with a dark cloud over them all the time? You know the type: Someone who is always pessimistic and views events that happen at work from a negative perspective. Or think of another person, one who has a short fuse and who everyone tiptoes around for fear of being on the receiving end of an angry e-mail, a slamming door, or something worse. How do we manage the emotions of these types of people so they change their behaviour and improve their performance?"

Before I had a chance to answer, Andrew carried on:

"This is where the competency of inspiring performance is so important, especially if we want to create a culture of high achievement. It is our ability to influence the moods and emotions of others and facilitate high performance through problem solving and promoting, recognising, and supporting the work of others. We also work with them to find effective ways of responding to events that upset them and provide assistance to resolve issues that are affecting their performance.

"People in the business have differing needs and are motivated by different things. They also have varying personality types that do not have the same priorities as you. So we have to be aware that what motivates us on an individual level may not be what motivates a team member," he added.

"I know that makes sense," I replied. "We have used DiSC in our organisation too, and it is noticeable how the four different personality styles are driven by different needs. This also helps us understand and manage conflict in the business between departments and create more harmonious teams. And looking at personality, it is also apparent that some leaders in my organisation are more capable of displaying the competencies of emotional intelligence than others, especially when it is about understanding how others feel. As leaders, it is important that we understand how our personality impairs or enhances our ability to act with emotionally intelligent behaviour while managing others. By doing this, we have a greater chance of inspiring high levels of performance in others and achieving great results."

"There is an important link between awareness of others and management of others," he noted. "They go hand in hand; if we are not aware, how can we manage? Research does suggest that in high-performing organisations, people feel significantly more engaged, cared for, valued, proud, and motivated than those in mediocre-performing organisations, where people feel fearful, stressed, and disempowered."

He continued, "Leadership is fundamentally about facilitating performance. There is a proven link between emotional intelligence and the capacity to facilitate emotions in others that drive high performance and increase employee engagement. This is more than just a moral compass; it's also a recipe for success. Organisations with emotionally intelligent leaders achieve a critical level of sustainable competitive advantage: a high-performance culture and customer loyalty."

"I hope your time here has provided you with insight into how important emotionally intelligent leaders are to the performance of your people," he said.

"It absolutely has, Andrew," I replied excitedly. "It's been a most worthwhile use of my time. I can now certainly see that there is a direct link between the way people feel and the way they perform. Most importantly, though, I can see that it is an area that can add significant value to the way I help my staff drive performance and transform the business from a good business to a great one."

"Before we applied the concept of emotional intelligence to our simple success formula—physical, mental, emotional—we really did not understand how our emotions impacted our capacity to work hard for long periods of time and enable us to deliver high quality for sustainable periods. It completed the relationship," he explained, "and enabled us to create a high-performing culture."

"Remember, though," he said, looking directly in my eyes, "education without action is entertainment. I am certainly not an entertainer. So seek feedback from others and find out how well you demonstrate the emotionally intelligent leadership competencies, then share and educate your leadership team and embed emotional intelligence into your organisation's culture."

He sought feedback from others in his organisation on his leadership capability.

They were asked:

1. How important it is to them that he displayed the competencies in question, and
2. How well he demonstrated the leadership competencies in question in comparison to others.

He checked in on a regular basis to see how he was feeling and acting at work to see if his emotions were enhancing or impairing his performance.

He made time to get to know those he worked with in more depth, exploring their values and beliefs, and identifying different personality styles, to become more aware of their feelings and motivations.

He took the time to record what he was feeling and made sure he expressed himself at the right time, to the right degree, to the right person, and in the right place.

He used both technical and emotional data when making decisions, considering his own and others perspective, explaining the rationale behind those decisions.

He utilised proactive and reflective techniques to manage and control his emotions and took the responsibility to choose his response to a given situation.

He inspired his team to transition from good to great by facilitating high performance through problem solving and promoting, recognising, and supporting the work of others.

He became an emotionally intelligent leader.

He inspired performance.

He ran a *great* organisation.

He slept more.

Tiredness makes cowards of us all.

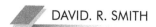

DAVID. R. SMITH

Emotional Intelligence in Summary

Emotional intelligence involves a set of skills that define how effectively you perceive, understand, reason with, and manage your own and others' feelings.		
EI Competency	**Definition**	**Workplace Outcomes**
Emotional Self-Awareness	The skill of perceiving and understanding your own emotions.	• The capacity to identify and understand the impact one's own feelings are having on decisions, behaviour and performance at work • Greater self-awareness
Emotional Awareness of Others	The skill of perceiving and understanding others' own emotions.	• Greater understanding of others and how to engage, respond, motivate and connect with them • Interpersonal effectiveness
Emotional Expression	The skill of expressing your own emotions effectively.	• Creating greater understanding amongst colleagues about yourself • Creating trust and perceptions of genuineness amongst colleagues

82

Emotional Reasoning	The skill of utilising emotional information in decision-making.	• Enhanced decision-making where different types of information are gathered and processed • Greater buy-in from others into decisions that are made.
Emotional Self-Management	The skill of effectively managing and controlling your own emotions.	• Improved job satisfaction and engagement • Improved ability to cope with high work demands • Enhanced productivity and performance • Improved emotional well-being • The capacity to think clearly in stressful situations • The capacity to effectively deal with situations that cause strong emotions
Inspiring Performance	The skill of facilitating high performance in others.	• The capacity to generate a positive and satisfying work environment for others • The capacity to deal with workplace conflict effectively • The ability to recognise, promote, and support others' work

APPENDIX

Your EI Leadership Success Profile

The profiler consists of forty-two questions, which are answered on an anchored rating scale. When completing the profiler, you should make note of the following points:

- There is no right or wrong response to any of the questions.
- The key to completing it accurately is to consider *How often do I need to display this behaviour to perform my role successfully?* each time you read one of the statements.
- It is important not to think of the way you behaved in one situation; rather, your response should be based on your *typical* behaviour.

The questions begin on the next page.

Answer Key:
1 = Significantly less than
2 = Less than
3 = Average/typical
4 = More than
5 = Significantly more than

Comparing yourself to other leaders you have worked with, indicate how well you believe you demonstrate the following:	Significantly Less	Less than	Average/typical	More than	Significantly More	N/A / not sure
1. Understanding the impact your behaviour has on others	1	2	(3)	4	5	X
2. Being aware of your strength and limitations	1	2	3	(4)	5	X
3. Asking others for feedback on your leadership	1	(2)	3	4	5	X
4. Responding effectively to feedback provided to you	1	2	3	(4)	5	X
5. Being consistent in what you say and do	1	2	(3)	4	5	X
6. Behaving in a way that is consistent with how you expect others to behave	1	2	(3)	4	5	X
7. Demonstrating awareness of your mood and emotions	1	2	(3)	4	5	X
SUM and divide by 7 to obtain an average score for Self-Awareness						
8. Making others feel appreciated	1	2	3	(4)	5	X
9. Adjusting your style so that it fits well with others	1	2	3	(4)	5	X
10. Noticing when someone needs support and responding effectively	1	2	3	(4)	5	X
11. Accurately viewing situations from the perspective of others	1	2	3	(4)	5	X
12. Acknowledging the views and opinions of others	1	2	3	(4)	5	X
13. Accurately anticipating responses or reactions from others	1	2	3	(4)	5	X
14. Balancing achieving results with others' needs	1	2	3	(4)	5	X
SUM and divide by 7 to obtain an average score for Awareness of Others						

15. Being open about your thoughts, feelings, and opinions	1	2	③	4	5	X
16. Expressing thoughts and feelings in a way that is sensitive to others	1	2	3	④	5	X
17. Facilitating robust, open debate	1	2	③	4	5	X
18. Being open and honest about mistakes	1	2	③	4	5	X
19. Honouring commitments and keeping promises	1	2	3	④	5	X
20. Encouraging others to put forward their thoughts, feelings, and opinions	1	2	3	④	5	X
21. Responding effectively when challenged	1	2	3	④	5	X
SUM and divide by 7 to obtain an average score for Authenticity						
22. Consulting others in decision-making	1	2	3	④	5	X
23. Explaining the rationale behind decisions you make	1	2	3	④	5	X
24. Involving others in decisions that affect their work	1	2	3	④	5	X
25. Considering issues from multiple perspectives	1	2	3	④	5	X
26. Taking the bigger picture into account when decision-making	1	2	3	④	5	X
27. Reflecting on feelings when decision-making	1	2	3	④	5	X
28. Making ethical decisions	1	2	3	4	⑤	X
SUM and divide by 7 to obtain an average score for Emotional Reasoning						

87

29. Effectively managing your emotions in difficult situations	1	2	③	4	5	X
30. Demonstrating a positive and energising demeanour	1	2	③	4	5	X
31. Managing your time effectively	1	2	3	4	⑤	X
32. Learning from your mistakes	1	2	3	4	⑤	X
33. Keeping up to date with industry trends and market conditions	1	2	3	④	5	X
34. Striving to improve your performance	1	2	3	④	5	X
35. Quickly adapting to new circumstances	1	2	3	④	5	X
SUM and divide by 7 to obtain an average score for Self-Management						
36. Providing useful support and guidance	1	2	3	④	5	X
37. Providing constructive feedback on behaviour and performance	1	2	3	④	5	X
38. Helping others understand their purpose and contribution to the organisation	1	2	3	④	5	X
39. Noticing inappropriate behaviour in others and responding effectively	1	2	3	④	5	X
40. Maintaining a positive work environment	1	2	3	④	5	X
41. Helping facilitate others to develop and advance their careers	1	2	3	④	5	X
42. Recognising others' hard work and achievements	1	2	3	④	5	X
SUM and divide by 7 to obtain an average score for Inspiring Performance						

Summarise Your EI Self-Assessment Scores

In the space provided below, enter your average scores for the six competencies of EI you obtained with the profiler.

Emotionally Intelligent Leadership Competency	Self-Assessed Result
Self-Awareness	
Awareness of Others	
Authenticity	
Emotional Reasoning	
Self-Management	
Inspiring Performance	

The table above shows the seven skills of EI and your average according to your own perspective. This information can be used to help set EI development goals by comparing it to actual assessment results. It can also be used to help consider which emotional intelligence skills you should focus most on.

My Development Goal

Describe a development goal that you would like to achieve with emotional intelligence.

....
....
....
....
....
....
....

Describe how you would measure the success of achieving this goal

....
....
....
....
....
....
....

Describe the benefits that might result from achieving this goal

....
....
....
....
....
....
....

Game changing for business.
Life changing for people.

For more information about Genos
Emotional Intelligence Assessments and
Trainings:

570-517-7100
rick@paramountbusinessdevelopment.com
admin@paramountbusinessdevelopment.com
paramountbusinessdevelopment.com

Helping businesses reach New HEIGHTS.

CPSIA information can be obtained
at www.ICGtesting.com
Printed in the USA
BVHW031849150419
545561BV00001B/48/P